Dear Lotté — Thank you
and M̶e̶r̶r̶y̶ ̶C̶h̶r̶i̶s̶t̶m̶a̶s̶!

D1239201

the Winiskele
Family
1996

Dietrich Bonhoeffer

The Mystery
of Holy Night

Edited by Manfred Weber

Translated by Peter Heinegg

A Crossroad Book

The Crossroad Publishing Company

New York

Foreword

On the first Sunday in Advent, 1943, Dietrich Bonhoeffer wrote from Tegel Prison in Berlin to his parents: "The Altdorfer [German painter Albrecht Altdorfer, 1480–1538— *trans.*] Nativity, which portrays the Holy Family at the manger amidst the ruins of a dilapidated house—whatever made him do that, 400 years ago, against all tradition?—is especially on my mind these days. Perhaps Altdorfer meant to tell us, 'Christmas can, and should, be celebrated in this way too.' In any event that's what he does tell us."

Ten years earlier, Dietrich Bonhoeffer was a pastor in London, where, on the third Sunday of Advent, 1933, he preached on the Magnificat (Luke 1:46–55). This sermon makes up the first part of this book. He wrote the commentary on Isaiah 9:6–7 in 1940 at the Benedictine monastery of Ettal as a sermon–meditation for pastors of the Confessing Church in Pomerania. The Christian message seeks to change people, to promote the reign of peace and justice. For Dietrich Bonhoeffer, the cross and the manger were crucial stages on the way to change. We have two highly personal bits of evidence concerning this experience of life and faith in the letter of December 17, 1943, to his parents (p. 3) and the poem "By benevolent powers" (pp. 46–47), which was written during Christmastime, 1944. We are invited to reflect on Christmas with Dietrich Bonhoeffer, and to experience the authenticity of his interpretations for our time and our lives.

In the pages that follow, brief excerpts and selected longer texts are interspersed with pictures in such a way that together and each in its own way tell *the mystery of Holy Night.*

Dietrich Bonhoeffer to His Parents

I don't have to tell you how greatly I long for freedom, and for all of you. But for decades you gave us such incomparably beautiful Christmases that my grateful memory of them is strong enough to outshine even this rather dark one. It is times like these that show what it really means to have a past and an inner legacy independent of the change of times and conditions. The awareness of being borne up by a spiritual tradition that lasts for decades gives one a strong sense of security in the face of all transitory distress… From the Christian point of view, spending Christmas in a prison doesn't pose any special problem. Most likely, a more meaningful and authentic Christmas is celebrated here by many people than in places where only the name of the feast remains. Misery, pain, poverty, loneliness, helplessness, and guilt have an altogether different meaning in God's eyes than in the judgment of men. God turns toward the very places from which humans tend to turn away. Christ was born in a stable because there was no room for him at the inn: A prisoner can understand all this better than other people. It's truly good news for him; in believing it, he knows he has been made a part of the Christian community that breaks down all spatial and temporal frontiers, and the walls of prison lose their meaning.

Luke 1, 46–55

And Mary said,
"My soul magnifies the Lord,
and my spirit rejoices in God,
my Savior, for he has regarded
the low estate of his handmaiden.
For behold, henceforth all generations
will call me blessed;
for he who is mighty
has done great things for me,
and holy is his name.
And his mercy is on those who fear him,
from generation to generation.
He has shown strength with his arm,
he has scattered the proud
in the imagination of their hearts,
he has put down the mighty
from their thrones,
and exalted those of low degree.
He has filled the hungry
with good things,
and the rich he has sent empty away.
He has helped his servant Israel,
in remembrance of his mercy,
as he spoke to our fathers,
to Abraham
and to his posterity for ever."

A Woman's Passionate Song

This song of Mary is the oldest Advent hymn.
It is at once the most passionate, the wildest,
and one might even say, the most revolutionary
Advent hymn ever sung.
This is not the gentle, tender, dreamy Mary
whom we sometimes see in paintings;
this is the passionate, surrendered,
proud, enthusiastic Mary who speaks out here.
This song has none of the sweet, nostalgic, or even playful tones
of some of our Christmas carols.
It is, instead, a hard, strong, inexorable song
about collapsing thrones and humbled lords of this world,
about the power of God and the powerlessness of humankind.
These are the tones of the women prophets
of the Old Testament
that now come to life in Mary's mouth.

Celebrating Advent Means Knowing How to Wait

Mary, grasped and seized by the Spirit,
speaks of God's coming into the world,
of the advent of Jesus Christ.
For she knows better than anyone what it means
to wait for Christ.
She waits for him in a way unlike anyone else.
She awaits him as his mother.
She knows about the mystery of his coming,
about the Spirit that is at play here,
about the almighty God who works his wonders.
She experiences in her own body
that God's ways with humans are wonderful,
that he isn't bound by human standards,
that he doesn't follow the path
that humans like to lay out for him—
that his way is beyond all understanding,
beyond all proof,
free, and with a mind of its own.

Where God Wants To Be

Where the understanding is outraged,
where human nature rebels,
where our piety keeps a nervous distance:
there, precisely there, God loves to be;
there he baffles the wisdom of the wise;
there he vexes our nature, our religious instincts.
There he wants to be, and no one can prevent him.
Only the humble believe him and rejoice
that God is so free and grand,
that he works wonders where man loses heart,
that he makes splendid what is slight and lowly.
Indeed, this is the wonder of wonders,
that God loves the lowly.
"God has regarded the low estate of his handmaiden."
God in lowliness—
that is the revolutionary, the passionate word of Advent.

A Christian's life does not consist in words,

but in experience.

No one is a Christian without experience.

That doesn't mean "life experience,"

but the experience of God.

———————

We have to become clear

in the presence of the manger in the stable of Bethlehem

how we want to think, from this point on,

about what is high and low in human life.

So long as there are men and women, Christ walks the earth

as your neighbor,

as the one through whom God calls on you, speaks to you,

and makes demands on you.

That is the most serious and

most blessed thing about the Advent message.

Christ lives in the shape of the person in our midst.

———————

Joy lives on silence

and on incomprehensibility.

God is not ashamed of human lowliness.

He enters right into it.

He chooses a human being to be his instrument

and works his wonders

where they are least expected.

––––––––––––––

Where else are we to seek mercy

for all our betrayals, all our weak faith,

all our failures,

but in the lowliness of God in the manger?

Those Who Go to the Manger Will Be Transformed

If God chooses Mary as his instrument,
if God himself wants to come into this world
in the manger at Bethlehem,
that is no idyllic family affair,
but the beginning of a complete turnaround,
a reordering of everything on this earth.
If we wish to take part in this Advent and Christmas event,
then we cannot simply be bystanders or onlookers,
as if we were at the theater,
enjoying all the cheerful images.
No, we ourselves are swept up into the action there,
into this conversion of all things.
We have to play our part too on this stage,
For the spectator
is already an actor.
We cannot withdraw.

What part, then, do we play?
Pious shepherds, on bended knee?
Kings who come bearing gifts?
What sort of play is this, where Mary becomes the mother of God?
Where God enters the world in the lowliness of the manger?
The judgment of the world and its redemption—
that is taking place here.
And the Christ child in the manger is himself the one
who pronounces the judgment and the redemption of the world.
He repels the great and the powerful.
He puts down the mighty from their thrones,
He humbles the arrogant,
his arm overpowers all the proud and the strong,
he raises what is lowly and makes it great and splendid
in his compassion.
Therefore we cannot approach his manger
as if it were the cradle of any other child.
Those who wish to come to his manger
find that something is happening within them.

Manger and Cross

For the mighty ones,
for the great ones of this world,
there are only two places
where their courage deserts them,
which they fear in the depths of their souls,
which they dodge and avoid:
the manger and the cross of Jesus Christ.

Celebrating Christmas

Who among us will celebrate Christmas right?
Those who finally lay down all their power, honor, and prestige,
all their vanity, pride, and self-will
at the manger,
those who stand by the lowly and let God alone be exalted,
those who see in the child in the manger the glory of God
precisely in this lowliness.
Those who say, along with Mary,
"The Lord has regarded my low estate.
My soul magnifies the Lord,
and my spirit rejoices in God my Savior."

If in Jesus Christ God stakes out a claim in the world—

even if only in a stable,

because "there was no room at the inn"—

then at a stroke he unites in this narrow space

the whole reality of the world

and reveals its ultimate foundation.

_____

Jesus Christ is the love of God become human

for all men and women,

and hence he is not a preacher

of abstract ethical ideologies,

but the concrete executor of the love of God.

Today, who can manage to wait,

to live in the future

as if it were the present,

to live on God

as if he were more certain than our own lives?

Only those who know

that the God who will come

has long since come before.

———————

In the birth of Jesus Christ

God took on humanity,

not just a single man.

If God has loved the world,

the whole of fallen creation,

then he gave us no preference over the others.

He has loved my worst enemy

no less than myself.

―――――――――

Where there is still hope, there is no defeat.

With God

dwells joy, and down from God it comes,

seizing mind, soul, and body;

and where this joy has grasped a human being

it spreads, it carries away,

it bursts through closed doors.

———————

If the earth has been found worthy

to bear the human being Jesus Christ,

if a person like Jesus has lived,

then and only then

does our human life make sense.

The joy of God has passed through

the poverty of the manger and the torment of the cross;

and so it is unconquerable, irrefutable.

———————————

The shepherds, like the wise men from the East,

stand at the manger,

not as "converted sinners," but simply because,

just as they are,

they have been drawn by the manger.

Isaiah 9, 6–7

For unto us a child is born,
unto us a son is given;
and the government shall upon his shoulder:
and his name shall be called
Wonderful, Counselor, Mighty God,
Everlasting Father, Prince of Peace.
Of the increase of his government
and of peace,
there shall be no end,
upon the throne of David,
and upon his kingdom,
to establish it, and to uphold it
with judgment and with justice
from this time forth and even for evermore.
The zeal of the LORD of hosts will do this.

The Lord of the Ages Is God

When the prophet speaks these words,
the time of fulfillment is still 700 years away.
But so deeply is the prophet immersed
in God's thoughts and decisions
that he speaks of what is to come as though he has seen it already,
that he speaks of the saving hour,
as if he has already stood in worship at the manger of Jesus.
"Unto *us* a child is born."
We who don't know what will happen next year,
how are we to understand
someone looking out over the centuries?
This voice of a single person,
gently ringing down through the ages
joined now and then by another isolated voice of prophecy,
chimes in at last with the shepherds' midnight adorations
and cries out in jubilation:
"For unto us a child is born, unto us a son is given."

The Turning Around of All Things

   We are talking about the birth of a child,
not the revolutionary act of a strong man,
not the breathtaking discovery of a sage,
not the pious act of a saint.
It really passes all understanding: The birth of a child
is to bring the great turning around of all things,
is to bring salvation and redemption to the whole human race.
What kings and statesmen, philosophers and artists,
founders of religions and moral teachers vainly strive for,
now comes about through a newborn child.

Everything Past and Everything Future

     As if to shame
the mightiest human efforts and achievements,
a child is placed at the center of history.
A child, born of humans: a son, given by God.
That is the mystery of the world's redemption.
Everything past and everything future is encompassed here.
The infinite mercy
of almighty God comes to us,
condescends to us in the form of a child, his son.
That this child has been born for *us*,
that this son has been given,
that this human child, this son of God, belongs to *me*;
that I know him, have him, love him,
that I am his and he is mine —
my very life now depends entirely on all these things.
A child has our life in his hand.

The Moment of Fulfillment

How do we wish to meet this child?
Have our hands become too hard and proud
from daily work
to fold themselves in adoration at the sight of this child?
Do we carry our head,
which has had to think so many heavy thoughts
and to solve so many problems,
too high for us to bow it humbly
before the wonder of this child?
Can we one more time forget entirely
all our strivings, accomplishments, and importance,
to join the shepherds and the sages from the East
and offer childlike adoration to the divine child in the manger?
To take, like old Simeon, this child in our arms
and instantly
acknowledge with gratitude the fulfillment of our entire life?
It is truly a strange sight
when a strong, proud man bends his knee before this child,
when with a simple heart he finds and reveres in him
his Savior.
And our old, clever, experienced, self-assured world
must no doubt shake its head, or perhaps even laugh with contempt,
when it hears the cry of salvation from believing Christians,
"For unto us a child is born, unto us a son is given."

God Is A God of Bearing

"And the government shall be upon his shoulder,"
The government of the world is supposed to lie
on the weak shoulders of this newborn child!
One thing we know:
These shoulders will in any event get to carry
the burden of the entire world.
With the cross, all the sin and distress of this world
will be loaded onto these shoulders.
But the government will consist,
not in the bearer's breaking down under the burden,
but in his bringing it to the goal.
The government that lies on the shoulders of the child
in the manger
consists in the patient bearing of humans and their guilt.
This bearing, however, begins in the manger,
begins where the eternal word of God
took on and bore human flesh.
Precisely in the lowliness and weakness of the child,
the government of all the world has its beginning.

Out of love for humans God becomes human.

———————

The reason for God's love of man or woman

lies not in man or woman, but only in God himself.

———————

God is closer to us than the past.

God's paths are the paths

that he himself has taken and that we now

are to take with him.

———————————

Had Jesus not lived,

our life, in spite of all the other people

whom we know, admire, and love,

would be meaningless.

A human life

is worth as much as the respect it holds

for the mystery.

————————

Grateful as we are for all personal joys,

not for a moment may we lose sight

of the great things

for the sake of which we are alive.

God doesn't want dead Christians, but Christians

who live unto their Lord.

Unless we hear this word,

Christmas will have passed us by.

———————————

The world can be renewed

only from the impossible;

this impossible is God's blessing.

One Single Name

Who is this child whom the prophets foretell
and over whose birth heaven and earth exult?
Only in stammering can one speak his name,
can one try to describe
what is encompassed in his name.
Words pile up and pour out in a rush when they are to say
who this child is.
Indeed, strange combinations of words, otherwise unknown to us,
come into being
when the name of this child
is to pass human lips:
"Wonderful Counselor," "Mighty God,"
"Everlasting Father," "Prince of Peace."
Every one of these words has endless depths,
and all of them together try
to express only one single name: Jesus.

Wonderful Counselor

"Wonderful Counselor" is the name of this child.
But because this child of God is God's own Wonderful Counselor,
he himself is a fountain of all wonders and all counsel.
For those who recognize in Jesus the wonder of the Son of God
his every word and deed becomes a wonder;
they will find in him the last, deepest, most helpful counsel
for all their trials and troubles.
Go to the child in the manger, believe in him the Son of God
and you will find in him
wonder upon wonder, counsel upon counsel.

Mighty God

"Mighty God" is the name of this child.
The child in the manger is none other than God himself.
Nothing greater could be said:
God became a child.
He lies in the manger, poor like us,
wretched and helpless like us,
a human of flesh and blood like us, our brother.
And yet he is God, yet he is strength.
Where is the divinity, where is the strength of this child?
In the divine love, in which he became just like us.
His poverty in the manger is his strength.
In the strength of love
he overcomes the chasm between God and humanity.

Everlasting Father

"Everlasting Father"—
How can this be the name of the child?
This child wants nothing for himself;
he is no *wunderkind* in the human sense,
but an obedient child of his heavenly Father.
Born in time, he brings eternity with him to earth.
As the Son of God
he brings us all the love of the Father in heaven.
Go there, seek and find at the manger the eternal Father,
who here has become your dear Father too.

Prince of Peace

"Prince of Peace"—
Where God comes in love to humans, unites himself with them,
peace is made between God and human being
and between human being and human being.
If you are afraid of God's anger, go to the child in the manger,
and get the peace of God as a gift.
Have you fallen into strife and hatred with your brother,
come and see how, purely from love,
God has become our brother
and wants to reconcile us, one with another.
Out in the world power rules.
This child is the prince of peace. Where he is, peace rules.

Implied in One Name

"Wonderful Counselor, Mighty God, Everlasting Father,
        Prince of Peace"—
That is how we speak at the manger in Bethlehem.
Our words rush out
at the sight of the divine child;
we try to put into language
what is implied in the one name: Jesus.
But at bottom these words are nothing
except a wordless silence of adoration
before the ineffable, before the presence of God
in the shape of a human child.

Peace and Justice

A kingdom of peace and justice,
the unfulfilled longing of humankind,
has dawned with the birth of the divine child.
We are called to this kingdom.
We can find it
if we accept the word and sacrament of the Lord Jesus Christ
in the church, in the community of the faithful,
and submit to his rule,
if we acknowledge our Savior and Redeemer
in the child in the manger
and let him give us the gift of a new life in love.
"From now on" means that from the birth of Jesus,
"until eternity," this kingdom will endure.
Who guarantees
that it will be not shattered and go under
amidst the storms of world history
like all other kingdoms?
"The zeal of the Lord of hosts will do this."
The holy zeal of God for his cause guarantees
that this kingdom will last to all eternity
and will come to its last fulfillment,
in spite of all human guilt, in spite of all resistance.

God is love.
That means that the beginning and the end of human life
are sheltered in God's hands.

———————

The fact that we are allowed to live
as real human beings
and to love the real person beside us,
is founded solely on the incarnation of God,
on the unfathomable love of God for humankind.

Faithfully and quietly surrounded by benevolent powers,
wonderfully guarded and consoled,
—thus will I live this day with you
and go forth with you into another year.

Still will the past torment our hearts
Still, heavy burdens of bad times depress us,
Ah, Lord, give our startled souls
the grace for which we were created.

And if you pass to us the heavy, the bitter
cup of pain, filled to the brim,
we will accept it, grateful, without trembling
from your good and beloved hand.

But if you wish us to rejoice once more
in this world and the brilliance of its sun,
then the past, too, we will remember,
and so our entire life will belong to you

With warmth and light let flame today the candles
that you have brought into our darkness.
If it can be, bring us together once again!
We know your light is shining in the night.

When the silence spreads around us deeply,
let us hear that full sound of the world
stretching out invisibly around us;
let us hear your children's praising song.

Warmly protected by benevolent powers,
with confidence we wait for what may come.
God is with us at evening and at morning
and most certainly at each new day.

About the Author:

Dietrich Bonhoeffer (1906-1945)

After work as a university chaplain and secretary of an ecumenical youth group, he went to London in 1933 to serve as a pastor because he saw no more options for himself in Germany. But in 1935 he returned and soon joined the anti-Hitler resistance. Arrested in 1943, he was sent to the Tegel military prison in Berlin, where he wrote the most important of his letters and sketches. On April 9, 1945, he was executed in the concentration camp at Flossenbürg.

Literary Sources:

Page 2: Dietrich Bonhoeffer, *Widerstand und Ergebung. Briefe und Aufzeichnungen aus der Haft*, ed. Eberhard Bethge. 1994. Eberhard Bethge, *Dietrich Bonhoeffer, Theologe-Christ-Zeitgenosse. Eine Biographie*. 1994.

Page 3, 22 (bottom), 32 (center), 33 (top and bottom), 35 (bottom), 46, 47: Dietrich Bonhoeffer, *Widerstand und Ergebung*.

Pages 6, 7, 14, 15, 16, 17: Dietrich Bonhoeffer, *Werke*, Vol 9. London 1933–1935, ed. Hans Goedeking, Martin Heimbucher, and Hans W. Schleicher. 1994.

Pages 10 (top), 19 (bottom), 20 (top and bottom), 26, 27, 28 30, 31, 32 (bottom), 35 (top), 36, 38, 39, 40, 42, 43, 44, 45 (top): Dietrich Bonhoeffer, *Predigten-Auslegungen-Meditationen*, 1935-1945, ed. Otto Dudzus. 1985.

Pages 10 (bottom), 11 (top and bottom), 12 (top and bottom), 19 (top): Dietrich Bonhoeffer, *Predigten*, etc.

Pages 22 (top), 23 (bottom): Dietrich Bonhoeffer, *Werk*, Vol. 6, *Ethik*, ed. Ernst Feil, Clifford Green, Heinz E. Tödt and Lise Tödt. 1992.

Pages 22 (top), 23 (bottom), *Dietrich Bonhoeffer Lesebuch*, ed. Otto Dudzus. 1994.

All the above-mentioned books have been published by the Chr. Kaiser/Gütersloher Verlagshaus. We thank the publisher for their kind permission to reprint the texts chosen.

List of Reprodutions:

Page 5: Annunciation, Fra Angelico/AKG
Page 9: Visitation, Dieric Bouts the Elder/AKG
Page 13: Birth of Christ, Stefan Lochner/bpk, Photo H. Buresch
Page 21: Birth of Christ, Albrecht Altdorfer/bpk, Photo Jörg P. Anders
Page 25: Annunciation to the Shepherds, Book of Hours of Jean Bourdichon/Gerstenberg Archives
Page 29: Adoration of the Shepherds, Lorenzo di Credi/AKG
Page 37: Adoration of the Magi, Giotto di Bondone/bpk
Page 41: Presentation in the Temple, Rogier van der Weyden/Artothek, Photo J. Blauel

1996
The Crossroad Publishing Company
370 Lexington Avenue, New York, NY 10017

Copyright © 1996 by Kiefel Verlag GmbH, Wuppertal/Gütersloh
English translation Copyright © 1996 by The Crossroad Publishing Company

All rights reserved. No part of this book may be reproduced, stored, in a retrieval system, or transmitted in any form or by any means, electronic, mechanical, photocopying, recording, or otherwise, without the written permission of The Crossroad Publishing Company.

Printed in Germany

Library of Congress Catalog Card No.: 96–85500

ISBN 0-8245-1591-9